Rhonda Joyce

mama's girl

My Journey to Overcoming the Spirit of Rejection

Published by Rhonda.ILLustrated
P.O. Box 1703
Spring Hill, TN 37174

Cover Design by Lisa Pearson
Cover Photo and Bio Headshot by Hillary Craig
Makeup by Samantha Fisher

Acknowledgements

First, I acknowledge Holy Spirit, The Spirit of Truth, my friend, and confidant. Thank You Holy Spirit, for leading me and guiding me through everything! You have always been constant in my life. Without You, I fail.

Dedication

This book is dedicated to the one person who has always added joy to my life. Alexandria, words really cannot describe what you mean to me. I love you. Thank you for being exactly who you are. We're in this together.

❧ Table of Contents ❧

Genesis: The Beginning

1 ◦ Yes Mama, Whatever You Say Mama!

10 ◦ No, Mama

18 ◦ Allie!

25 ◦ Hurt People Hurt People

Getting to the Root of the Mess

32 ◦ It's Complicated

39 ◦ Lilly's Mama

How I Broke the Chains

47 ◦ Chain Breakers

66 ◦ Plot Twist

How I Overcame

73 ◦ Overcoming: The New Testimony

90 ◦ A Final Word

93 ◦ Meet the Author

❧ Genesis: The Beginning ❧

"When you were born I couldn't stand to look at you because you looked so much like Mama. I had to learn to love her so that I could love you."
                                        - My Mama

❧ Yes Mama, Whatever You Say Mama! ❧

I'VE ALWAYS BEEN A MAMA'S GIRL, but not in the way you think.

First, let me share two of my earliest memories.

One Halloween while we were living in Michigan, my parents, my five siblings, and I had gone trick-or-treating and I got lost. I was probably around two years old at the time. I had been told not to eat my candy, but like any other child tempted with a goody bag, I couldn't wait. I stopped to dip into that bag. Now, I said I got lost, but I think it's more accurate to say they lost me. One minute, I was with the group and the next minute I was out on the sidewalk by myself crying. A man and woman appeared and asked me if I belonged to the Major. I answered yes. The Major, a major in the U.S. Army, was my biological father. The couple brought me to the apartment house where my family lived. I remember going through the building's front door, then someone opened the front door to my family's apartment. I vaguely remember that they handed me to my mother.

The next memory that I have is of our family living in Nashville, TN. I do not remember my exact age but I was around four. At this time, I was called by my middle name: Joyce. When I became a teenager, I requested that everyone call me Rhonda. I decided my first name was more to my liking. Anyway, it was at that moment that I realized my existence in the world. I realized at this point that I was a person who had brothers, sisters, and a mom. I understood that I, Rhonda Joyce, was a person who was alive and had the knowledge of who I was in relation to others.

Those two memories, though seemingly random, may help you understand where I'm coming from as you read. The memory of being lost by my family and recognizing that I exist in relation to others have become a theme in which I have learned who I am and why I'm here.

Now that I've explained that, I realize I've always been a Mama's Girl. This was not in the "most-beloved" of her daughters or the "apple of her eye" kind of Mama's Girl. I was the youngest of four girls, and for pretty much most of my life, I have been called Baby Girl. I was attached to my mother's hip. Admittedly, I was very much a cry baby. And as little sisters often do, if something went down, I would be the first one to run and tell Mama what happened. I did as she said because that's what I was taught. I knew the scripture Exodus 20:12 by heart. *"Honour thy* *father and thy mother: that thy days may be long upon the land which the L*ORD *thy God giveth thee.*" Because I did as I was taught, there was also much respect and honor given to my Mama. I was the homebody that didn't want to stray too far away from home. All of these things helped to develop me into the *Yes-Mama-Whatever-you-say-Mama-I'll-do-whatever-you-tell-me-to-do-Mama,* kind of Mama's Girl that I became.

One of my earliest memories of being a Mama's Girl was during our "swimming lessons." During the summer months, my mother would take us swimming at a local community park called Hadley Park. All seven of us would climb out of my mother's brownish-tan station wagon and converge upon the pool area. We would play, jump, and splash around in the three feet of water. Mom would be on the side of the pool beckoning.

"Come here," she'd say, "I'm going to teach you how to swim."

Naturally, I'd go to her. She'd put me on her legs and say, "Kick your legs and move your arms like you are swimming." So I'd kick my legs and move my arms. I would do this for a few minutes with her encouraging me. Then she would drop her legs and I'd end up sputtering and sinking in the water. This would happen time and time again. One day I complained to one of my sisters and she said, "Why do you think that we stay away from her?" My thought was, *why didn't someone clue me in to what was going on?* Afterwards, I remember telling her when she called me to lie across her knees that she was just going to dump me in the water. She would deny it every time.

"You can trust me," she'd say.

I had this blind trust in my mother so when she told me that she wouldn't dump me in the pool again, I believed her. I realize now that this was her way of "teaching" me but her method just made me more afraid of the water. Needless to say, I was so traumatized by her so-called lessons that I didn't learn to swim until I took professional swimming lessons as an adult. Saying no wasn't even a thought. She was my mother and everyone is supposed to trust their mothers and fathers, correct? After all, they do have our best interests at heart. Don't they?

My mother did have my best interest at heart when it came to salvation, however. I was introduced to Jesus as a young girl of about seven or eight years of age. One day my mother was combing my hair and it was just her and me alone in the room. She had begun to part and section my hair and then she said, "Say thank You, Jesus."

I repeated after her, "Thank You Jesus."

"Say it again," she commanded.

I didn't realize she wanted me to keep going. But if I stopped she told me to say it again and again. I didn't know why I was saying it. I just obeyed what she told me to do. As I was growing up and even into adulthood, she often said, "My Mama put a Bible in my hand. I can do no less than put one in each of my children's hands." She meant that literally. She would gather all six of us into her bedroom, and we would read the Bible. Each one of us was instructed to find a passage to read. One-by-one, we would take our turns. As we continued to read, Mama would fall asleep. Whoever was reading at the time would test the waters by stopping. If Mama said something, we knew, of course, that she wasn't asleep and that we needed to continue to read. After a length of time, the reader would stop and most of the time there would be no second response from Mama so we would gather our Bibles and tip out of the room. My grandmother gave my mother the gift of knowing Jesus. In turn, she passed it down to us. There would be other things, both good and bad, yet not visible to the naked eye, that were passed down generationally. It's only as I write these pages and revisit the notes with new eyes that I have been able to connect the dots.

Years passed and I continued to grow and mature into a young woman. One day, when I was about sixteen years old, Mama and I had a conversation that was a pivotal moment in my life. I was standing in the living room with my mother as we gathered items to give away. She looked at me and out of the blue she said, "When you were born I couldn't stand to look at you because you looked so much like Mama. I had to learn to love her so that I could love you." I was already battling low self-esteem, low self worth, and all of the other things that go along with being an awkward, self-conscious teenager. I looked back at her.

"You could have kept that to yourself. Why would

you tell me something like that?" I asked.

"I don't feel like that now," she said. "I'm over feeling that way." Then she went on about her business while I was left standing there stunned. Maybe she needed to confess that to get it off her chest. But whatever the reason, the cat was now out of the bag. That conversation ended and I went on about my business as best as I could considering the heavy load that I felt had been dropped into my psyche.

Even though Mama had released this burden that she had been carrying and said that she was over it, there was something still there and it manifested itself at different times. Her mouth said, *I'm over it,* but her behavior seemed to say that she still harbored some unspoken negative feelings towards me. Either that or there was just something about me that made her react differently in her interactions with me. If I go by what she said about not being able to look at me because I looked like my grandmother, then it's reasonable to guess that they had some serious issues. I sometimes wonder what happened between them that caused Mama to dislike her own mother, and thus, me. And why did her dislike skip my other siblings and only show up towards me like that?

In writing this, I have a memory of sitting under the kitchen table as a toddler, crying and pulling my hair. I'm not a psychologist, but I'm sure that was a response to stress or anxiety, or a negative emotion that I was feeling internally. I don't know what triggered it, but I may know a key person in my life who may have been a contributor. I continued being a Mama's Girl; honoring her and accommodating her in whatever thing she was asking of me.

I must let you know that my life wasn't all bad and that every encounter that I had with my mother was not a battleground. We had some differences as well as some similarities as do most mothers and daughters. I am, after all, the fruit of her womb. Although her wit could be sharp and hurtful at times, we shared a sense of humor. We loved the Lord as she raised all of her children to do. She loved her puzzle books and I loved to read. I would walk to the public library and stay for hours. I loved books and there were plenty to check out and take home. In fact, during my teenage years, whenever she punished me she would revoke my public library privileges as this was my go-to place.

I continued to be meek and submissive and obedient. I was not a rebellious child by any means. I liked peace and non-confrontational interactions. Mom has always been fiercely independent and she had a *my-way-or-the-highway* mentality. It was what it was. This may sound harsh, but this is the reality of some of her characteristics. My mother has always been a strong, independent, determined, and a somewhat opinionated woman. I say that in the sense that once her opinion has been established, that's pretty much the way it is. And because of that combination of traits, she usually got whatever it is that she wanted. We are both strong-willed, but I can be persuaded if the facts are present and undeniable. She, on the other hand, is not only stubborn, but she has a gift of persuasion and that spirit of manipulation that pops up from time to time. It's not a good combination. Children, even adult children, sometimes have a hard time admitting that at times, our parents are manipulative and that they do pull the "I'm the parent" trump card to get what they want from their children.

One day, there was a verbal altercation that transpired and she basically told me that I needed to move out. I was more than ready to go. I had started to foresee my future self living a spinster life of running all of Mama's errands forever and decided that that wasn't how I was going to live my life. I had to save myself. Needless to say, I didn't fight her on it.

After I moved into my own place, I would still visit Mama, bring groceries, or just to take her here or there. While at her house, for the most part we would get along great when it was just the two of us. There was good conversation or just sitting and watching TV together. Mama was still controlling, even from a distance. But yes, even though I'd moved out, I was still Mama's Girl. It's just the way I was wired. I loved my mother and had a hard time saying no to whatever she asked of me. I didn't want to disappoint her so I continued to go along with everything. I had a desire to please my Mama and to obey. I had learned in my childhood what happened when I didn't obey what she said and it was not pretty! I still had that *yes-Mama-whatever-you-say-Mama* mentality. I'm sure that she liked it. I cannot say that I did, but it was all that I had known my whole life. But then my season changed. A man came into my life. He was someone who I was not expecting and I was willing to see where the relationship would go. Many young women desire to be married and have a family, and I was no different. Just think about it. Who wants to be alone and lonely, living at home with her Mama and some cats? There may be some of you who welcome the prospect, but I certainly did not. The season would again change for me and for my relationship with Mama.

∻ No, Mama ∼

T HE MAN'S NAME WAS ISAAC. Now, he was not truly the issue. But then again maybe he was. I had moved out and was making my way in the world as Rhonda, not Mama's Girl. I graduated again from college with a Bachelors of Science in Nursing and had become a Licensed Registered Nurse. Even with that accomplishment, I carried the same esteem issues I'd been having from my younger years. I was now in my late twenties and was still experiencing a lack of confidence and low self-esteem. My self-image was poor and I felt that I didn't have any value as a human being. I thought I'd never be married or have a child. I had no relationship prospects. I was not even in a relationship with God. I was not out in the streets, but I didn't know Him. Over the years, I gradually came to understand it was possible to go to church every week and still not have a relationship with Jesus. So there was no man and no Jesus. Frankly, I didn't see any permanent relationships in my future.

And then there was Isaac. All of a sudden and unexpectedly, at that, some of my co-workers began to tell me that there was this guy who wanted to meet me. I had seen Isaac around the nursing home but did not have an interest in him like that. I had enough sense to ask a couple of our mutual close friends if he was a good guy. I trusted what they said because they had known him longer than I had. After the stamp of approval from my friends, we began to talk and went out to dinner. We began spending time together. I wouldn't necessarily say that he was fun, but we got along well and he showed interest in me. For someone who was deceived by the enemy into thinking that they had no value, it was better than being alone.

To make a long story short, my interest was piqued. We kept talking and spending even more time together, and guess what happened? You're correct! I got pregnant. My first reaction upon realizing that I was pregnant was disbelief. I took three pregnancy tests to confirm it and they all read the same thing! How silly was that? I had always wanted children but this was not the way that I desired it to be. I wanted to be married. I certainly didn't want to be another statistic of an unwed mother raising a child by herself. After realization sunk in that I was really pregnant, I had mixed emotions. I was excited that I was pregnant, but I was also devastated because I had allowed myself to get into this situation.

At first, Isaac was excited about the pregnancy, but something shifted. Even though he had promised that he would take care of and support our baby, his enthusiasm quickly fizzled as the months progressed.

There was never a moment, however, in which I didn't want the pregnancy. It was simply not the way that I envisioned myself bringing my child into this world. My unborn child deserved both a full-time mother and a father in his or her life. I had seen enough single parent homes to know that this was not the route that I wanted to take. When the shock and devastation wore off, the excitement overtook my other emotions and I was elated that I was going to have a baby. It was during this time, I learned that Isaac had other fish in the pond and the pie crust promises that he easily made were also easily broken. I knew that the predicament that I was in was a result of me following my own plans. I didn't want to be alone. I wanted that special someone. But God's will would not include premarital sex. Yet, my baby was a blessing.

After that I had to figure out life with a new baby and no support. When Isaac realized that I was not going to carry additional dead weight, he ghosted me. It was just my baby, who I already absolutely adored, and me.

In the meantime, Mama decided that there was a way to handle this delicate situation of having a child out of wedlock. She was an ordained minister who knew all the rules and church etiquette.

"You need to go before the church and confess your sins and repent," she said. That's what she had been taught, so she was passing that tradition down the generational bloodline. But I was in my late twenties, liking the feel of independence from Mama, and certain that was not how I was going to play this thing out. I flat out refused.

"No."

I was not going to air my dirty laundry before the whole congregation. Quite frankly, in my estimation it was none of their business. I didn't sin in front of the church, and I was certainly not about to go before those people to repent. I had sinned against God and my own body, not the church folk. They were not the ones that I needed to seek forgiveness from. It was God who I needed to forgive my sin of fornication. The premarital sex was the sin, not the pregnancy. The pregnancy, however, was the result of the sin. Of course, that didn't sit well with Mama.

I didn't give in to Mama's requests that I needed to repent before the church. I had always thought that there was too much judgment by the people, the Body of the Church. Others have felt ostracized and left because they were not shown the love of God when they missed the mark.

But I was certain of one thing: I had to get in the position that God wanted me to be in. I had been going to church faithfully, sang in the choir, directed the choir and taught Sunday school, and still was jacked up in my thinking. I took the mandatory six weeks off from church even though I could have gone back sooner, I honestly didn't want to face the people because of my sin. For those who are wondering, I sat myself down from all ministry positions after I found out that I was pregnant. I stuck to my convictions though. I was not going before the church like that!

Maybe I was extra hormonal with the pregnancy or self-preservation began to kick in, but a few months before my daughter was born, I realized there were some things I had to put a stop to. I had begun to keep my distance from my own mother. It was not simply a physical distance. I began creating an emotional wall that preceded my ability to say no. She was no longer Mama. She was Lilly. In all I've said so far, it should be clear that this is not my demeanor. I love people. I love my Mama.

But one of the problems I had was that I have always felt that I was at the bottom of the food chain with Mama. This is my special lingo to describe the hierarchy in the family amongst the six children that my mother birthed. Even though she'd say, "I don't pick favorites. I treat all of my children the same," it felt as though some children were favored over the others. And it is entirely possible that this was not intentional, though the effect was the same. I felt like I was the least of them; the one lost on that Halloween night so many, many years ago. I never thought that it was my sibling's fault, and I place blame on not a single one of them. None of us were responsible for Mama's behavior.

To understand what I mean when I say I was at the bottom of the sibling food chain, you have to understand that there were specific behaviors that were aimed specifically towards me.

For example, Mama enjoyed receiving gifts and took great delight in trying to guess what was in the beautifully wrapped box. I would buy Mama gifts for her birthday and Christmas. One particular year, I brought her a nice jogging suit. She unwrapped the box and looked at it.

"That's really nice." She then turned to my sister Judy, passing her the box.

"You can have it," she said to her. I was literally speechless. I had saved my little money and I knew that she wanted something just to wear around the house but I didn't make a big deal out of it. There was another occasion in which I bought her a sweater for her birthday. She had said a couple of weeks prior that she would like a sweater. So being mindful of that, I went to a women's store and found what I thought was a nice sweater for her. She took it out of the gift box.

"I can't use it because my chest will be out." Once again she turned to the same sister.

"Here Judy, you can have it." I was so hurt. It wasn't just the fact that she gave the items away, but that she didn't even wait until I had left! After that, I didn't buy Mama any more gifts. The rejection stung.

From that moment on I started putting birthday and Christmas money in a card. I am very particular about the cards that I buy. They have to fit the person precisely. It was always interesting to watch Mama's reaction when she would get a card. She would put her legs together with the expectation that money would fall out. For a while, it did. And she would read the words afterward. But I wanted to change things up sometimes. I felt that it didn't take a lot of thought to give money as gifts but I felt that Mama left me no choice. I would sometimes also buy her a reusable container with different kinds of fruit and make it into a beautiful bowl. Mama loved fruit so I knew that she would like this gift. And she did. Thank God. Rejection averted. Our relationship was complex.

There was a specific thing that Mama had a habit of doing that reactivated and pressed that rejection button inside me. I didn't appreciate it at all. I'd visit her and everything would be fine. We'd be having an interesting conversation or we'd be laughing about something. Then another member of the family would come and she would start this behavior of laughing at me, talking about me, and making fun of me like I wasn't sitting there. The scripture that I lived by required I honor my mother. But another scripture comes to mind that says *"Fathers don't provoke your children to anger."* I don't know if it was anger I was experiencing, but I was hurt, confused, and sad. Prior to having my baby, I would end up crying and leaving.

One day, I decided that it was time to address the behavior.

"We're fine when we're by ourselves, but when

someone else comes around I become the brunt of your jokes and your proverbial punching bag." She listened to what I had to say and I noticed something interesting. She never acknowledged the behavior, but it stopped for a season. One day, she tried to pick it back up again.

"No," I said. "We're not going back to that."

In classic form, when I put a stop to things she did not like it so she found other ways to attempt to control me. I wouldn't necessarily say that she would get back at me. Mama was not what I would call vindictive by any means. But she did have a way of proving her point to her advantage and getting her way.

The truth was that I was tired of her behavior and the emotional bullying and the picking that I was subjected to when other people were around. When I stopped coming around and began to build that wall between us, I was running away from the emotional pain that I perceived my mother was inflicting on me. But it was more than a perception, it was my reality.

❧ Allie! ❧

AND THEN AFTER THE FULL FORTY WEEKS of an uncomplicated pregnancy, my baby, Allie arrived; all seven pounds and twenty-one inches of her! Mama mode kicked in immediately.

One wintry afternoon, however, I came in the door with her. She was just a tiny newborn less than three months old. I remember putting her down on the floor in her carrier and laying out on the floor crying out to God. I loved and adored her so this moment was not about her. I was beyond overwhelmed because of the condition of my heart and because of how far away from God I had positioned myself.

"This is not your best for me!" I cried.

I was hurt by Isaac's departure but I realized he perpetuated the exact thing that was done to him by his daddy. He, too, disappeared. I understand that now. I also realized that outside influences caused him to believe the horror stories about how bad "baby mamas" are. As some women are, I was lumped unjustly into this big category which was unfair. I didn't understand it at the time. And while it was very painful and difficult to accept, Isaac truly wasn't God's best for me. This fact had to be acknowledged and confessed through my tears.

"This is not how you want me to live my life!" I cried.

This is not to say that God's hand has not been on me, because things could have been much worse. I recognize that what He allowed, He had a purpose for. God never wastes anything that we go through and most times it is not even for us. It is for someone else who needs a word of faith and encouragement from the Lord. I confess that I am very thankful for God's intervention because if He had not moved people out of my life, I know that I would not have the relationship that I now have with God.

When I came back to church after the birth of my daughter, Allie, I felt led by the Holy Spirit to rededicate myself to God. I knew that I was saved, that I had given my heart and my life to Jesus. I also knew I had lost my way due to the poor decisions I'd made. Thankfully, all hope was not lost because I was able to make the turn back to Jesus. And Jesus in His infinite love forgave me and restored me back to Himself.

I adjusted quickly to my role as a single, new mom to a beautiful baby girl. I was able to stretch my maternity leave out so that I could stay at home with the baby for four months. She was breastfed for the first three months so although she was held by family and friends, no one else was able to feed her. During these days I fed her breast milk for nourishing her body, but I also fed her food for the nourishing of her spirit: love and sweet words and biblical declarations about who she is. I believe that this allowed for a special bond between the two of us. I learned through this experience that friends and acquaintances are quick to give advice about what to do and how to do it. Thankfully, God had given me discernment so that I knew what advice to accept and what advice to reject. On one particular visit to see Mama, she made a comment regarding the fact that Allie and I didn't really fraternize much with others.

"This is pitiful. This baby is three months old and I haven't even changed a diaper."

I thought that was an odd thing to say, but then I realized that not only had I confidently stepped into this new mom role, I was so ecstatic that I didn't mind taking care of all of the baby's needs on my own. In my younger years, "confident" was not typically a word that I would use to describe myself. Looking back, I see what God was doing with me: building me up to be the Rhonda I would be today. I wasn't complaining about the poopy diapers or feedings every two or three hours. I relished each moment because I was so grateful to have her. And she was a beautiful baby. When she had gotten older, I told her that I prayed every day asking God to please let me not have an ugly baby. And when I looked at her in the nursery window after she was cleaned up, I could not believe that this was my baby and how beautiful she was.

After the birth of my daughter, I noticed that Mama and I didn't clash so much. After I had rededicated my life to Christ, I began allowing the Holy Spirit to direct me more and more. I began to grow spiritually and gain mental strength. I had peace. There was a defining moment when I had to let her know that I wasn't going to continue to blindly obey what she was instructing me to do just because it was what she wanted. I still respected and honored her, but I was gaining spiritual maturity and breaking the control Mama had had over me a little more each day. It may not even be that she was changing, but I surely was. Setting boundaries for her and honoring her were not exclusive of one another. Boundaries and honor can, indeed, coexist.

One day, however, it reached the point where she had once again pushed the boundaries with her "guidance."

"The Holy Spirit is in control of my life. I am going to do what the Holy Spirit is telling me to do," I declared. I had the revelation that God was allowing this little person that depended upon me for every one of her needs, to give me strength. Because my first instinct was to protect her, I was able to stand up to anybody. Even my mother. The mama bear in me roared and she roared loudly!

It should have ended there. But it didn't. Mama called me one winter evening and she said, "I need you to go to the mall. Come get the keys and go help so-and-so do whatever."

"The baby's asleep and it's cold outside," I said. I knew that I didn't want to take myself or my baby out in the cold. Surely that was enough to deny her request, right?

"She can go back to sleep," Mama insisted.

"You want me to wake my baby and take her out in this cold to help somebody who didn't make a wise decision?!" I asked.

She then began the tactic of sweet talking me into going. Initially, I actually agreed. I didn't have a garage so I went outside to heat the car, came back inside, and put the baby's snowsuit on. I looked at her lying in her crib with this snowsuit on and I felt something shift inside of me.

I thought, *What am I doing? It's extremely cold outside. It's ten o'clock at night, if not later, and my baby is asleep. No! I'm not doing this.*

I went outside and turned the car off. Then I came back inside, took the baby's coat off, and settled her in her crib. Thankfully, she had stayed asleep the whole time. After that I picked up the phone and called Mama.

"I'm not coming out in the cold. My baby is warm and asleep and I was not going to risk her getting sick by bringing her out in the cold."

She was not happy. She attempted for a few minutes to talk me into coming out but I wasn't budging this time. Protecting my daughter was my main objective at all times. She hung up the phone to find someone else who was willing to brave the cold. With that refusal I began to feel stronger immediately. Power that had been slowly drained and relinquished was now coming back to its rightful owner. You have to remember that I have always been a "yes-mama-whatever-you-say-Mama" girl. I didn't tell her no very often. In fact, I rarely told her no. But if saying no meant Allie was safe, then that's what it had to be.

Allie's birth gave me a level of courage that I had not had and frankly I didn't know that I had. I could fight for her. Fighting for her gave me the boost of strength that I needed to fight for myself. She was a blessing that came out of a nonexistent relationship, out of nothingness. I never imagined that I would have her. My daughter would never have to guess whether or not she was loved or of value to my life. My actions towards her would demonstrate the love that I will forever have for her. My daughter was not the only new person to be birthed during this time. A new Rhonda emerged out of the birth of Allie, the indescribable blessing in disguise. I had yet to realize that I would be the generational curse breaker in my bloodline. The LORD would work through me to stop behaviors and patterns that generations past engaged in. Some of this was because they did what they were taught to do without questioning anything that was said. But this was not how my story was going to be told and it started with me standing boldly and saying no to Mama. I was able to do so because of this little bundle of pure joy that loved me unconditionally. She saved my life and I am eternally grateful for that.

❧ Hurt People Hurt People ❧

DURING THOSE EARLY DAYS, I realized I had to choose Rhonda and Baby Alllie. Mama needed to be at more than arm's length. I needed miles of distance from her and sometimes the miles between our homes was not enough, hence creating that emotional wall where I had no choice but to see her and differentiate her as Lilly, a woman, and not Mama. I still visited, though less frequently. I still shopped for her. She still called and asked me to run errands for her. Some visits were smoother than others. Some were more volatile with me leaving the negative environment in search of my peace. There were choices that had to be made and the reality is that when we are rejected by someone that we care deeply about, we are so emotionally involved that it is hard for us to think clearly and make rational decisions. So separation was necessary.

The plain fact is that hurt people hurt people. They may not even know that they are hurt because they've never dealt honestly with their issues, nor have they been healed from them. Still, I knew one thing: I was not going to subject my daughter to any of that harsh, hurtful treatment and rejection. In fact, at that point, I separated myself from it entirely.

The separation would be short-lived, yet effective in many ways. I hadn't yet delivered but I knew that I would have to go back to work. I needed to find a babysitter for Allie so when the time came everything would be in place.

Ms. Christie was an elderly woman who lived nearby who cared for many of the children in the neighborhood. I contemplated whether or not this was where I would take my Allie. Ms. Christie was not only nearby, but affordable. I was the working poor so while I had money to pay my bills, I would not be able to afford an expensive daycare for a four-month-old. Breastfeeding was easy and obviously free, but I had weaned Allie in preparation for me returning to work. I also now had to buy baby formula. Although the relationship with my mother was brittle, I still made the effort to go see her occasionally and to call her. As was her practice, she continued to communicate with me whenever she needed me to shop for her. Although I knew that Lilly was available, we were not on the good terms that we needed to be on for me to feel comfortable in asking her to watch my daughter. I was still hurting. As far as I'm aware, if Lilly noticed anything different in my behavior towards her, she didn't mention it to me. Regardless of how I was treated, I loved my mother. I just wasn't too fond of some of her attitudes and behaviors towards me.

One day, a friend stopped by my house for a quick visit. She told me that she had had a dream about me and that I was holding on to something that was basically hindering my progress in moving forward.

"What you're seeking is right in front of you," she said. Right away, I knew what she was referring to. It was the disconnect that I had made in my heart towards my Mama. I knew that there was a hardness there because I could feel it. After she said it, I reacted to her comment with immediate conviction, repentance, and tears. My heart began to release the resentment, the hurt, the pain, and the bitterness that I had been harboring against her. The reality was that I was the one who allowed the hurt to enter my spirit. Once there, it began to grow and fester into these other things that were not good for me. I was just so fed up with all of the rejection and the laughing at me and being talked about like I was a big joke to her.

Mama has always been a wise woman. The irony of this wisdom was that one of the things that she would say was, "You're not responsible for how people treat you, but you are responsible for how you treat them." This thought came to my mind. I could not control how she treated me, but with God's help I could control how I responded to her. I decided to let it go.

Shortly afterwards, Mama and I had a conversation. In the midst of the conversation, she asked me what I was going to do about childcare and I told her that I was thinking about asking Ms. Christie to watch my Allie. Mama snapped.

"If you let her watch the baby, I will call the authorities on her! She's old and doesn't need to be watching anybody's children!" This was more of my mother's manipulative behavior revealing itself because she didn't want anyone else to watch her grandchild. Ms. Christie was an innocent person who just loved children. She didn't deserve to get harassed because Lilly didn't approve of the decisions that I was making to protect my own child. I did not take Lilly's words lightly, I knew that she would carry them out to get her way. I also knew what I needed to do. I allowed some time to pass so that my emotions were under control and one day during a conversation I asked Mama how much she would charge me to watch Allie while I worked.

"I'll have to think about it," she said. I later learned that she was happy that I had asked her to watch the baby. We were able to move on from there once I let go of the hurt and anger and allowed God to heal my heart. This was not an instant change nor was it a quick process. However, I could not and am not able to hold onto a grudge. I call it a gift because it really is a blessing. I would always forget that I was supposed to be mad and start talking to the person. Later in life, I learned that this was a good characteristic to have. I mention this because being hurt is different from holding a grudge. There was pain, anger, hurt, and some resentment in my heart from years of rejection although I didn't recognize it as rejection until later.

Some might ask, "Why didn't you talk to her about what you were feeling?" The truth is, I did. I communicated to her the hurt that I felt on many different occasions. One day I told her, "Mothers are supposed to love unconditionally. You put all these conditions on your love." Looking back, my mother never admitted to doing any of the things that I expressed to her on many different occasions. She would go silent, and then her attitude would change for a while. I got to the point where I was just glad that the foolishness would stop even if it was temporary. I had long ago stopped expecting a deep conversation about why she acted the way she did. How do you have a conversation with a person that refuses to acknowledge their actions? There were just so many secrets and things that we didn't talk about. Honestly there are many aspects of her life that we can only speculate about because they were never discussed.

I'll spare you some of the details but I'll share what was important to know in order to get to the root of the mess, how I broke these chains and bonds, and how I overcame it. This is something that I will not pass on to my daughter. This generational curse of mother-daughter dysfunction was over for me and mine!

As I said, things didn't change overnight or become entirely peaceful between Mama and me. But the balance of power shifted.

Do you want to know the secret?

No one can overpower the Holy Spirit. I credit no one but Jesus. I don't know about her, but He changed me. In fact, the more I prayed for God to change the people in my life, I noticed that I was the one changing. Hallelujah! I say it often and it is absolutely true, when the Holy Spirit comes in, something else has to shift!

There were no answers to our longstanding issues that can simply be found in the present. Getting to the root of a problem involves question-asking, research, and observation of the past and present. Most importantly, it involves Holy Spirit revelation.

❧ Getting to the Root of the Mess ❧

"Again the kingdom of heaven is like a merchant seeking beautiful pearls, who when he had found one pearl of great price, went and sold all that he had and bought it."

Matthew 13:45-46, NKJV

❧ It's Complicated ❦

THE THING IS, I'M SURE I've already made it clear that I love my Mama and she loves us. However, there is so much more to her than being Mama. She was good at mothering us because whatever she decided to do, she did well. But Mama was also Lilly, a daughter, a sister, a woman, a wife, an ordained minister, a person with her own history. Her history would give me enough insight to understand only now what had previously transpired and what was happening between us.

Lilly was valedictorian of her class. She'd chosen not to go to college and she gave away a scholarship. I recently learned from digging into the family history that she didn't feel that she was smart enough to go to college even though she was at the top of her class. At the same time, she decided to forgo her schooling to obtain the family that she had always wanted. The end result: a husband, four girls and two boys. Despite her feelings of educational inadequacy, she always encouraged us to get an education.

"Go get you a college degree," she'd say. "It's alright to be married but you need to know how to take care of yourself if something ever happened to your husband. And over the years we did just that. All of Mama's children have either college degrees or have graduated from technical school. What or who made her believe she wasn't smart enough to go to college? I don't know.

Lilly never worked much outside the home except for odd jobs cleaning or sewing for a few people when I was younger. She had two husbands that I know of; both of them deceased. My biological father, The Major, worked at a car manufacturing plant. I didn't know him because we had moved away from Michigan and were living in Tennessee at the time of his death. Plus I was so young that I didn't remember him. I can still recall the time when Mama told us that he had died. The short story was that he was fishing and drinking in a boat and that he drowned. I recently found out that because he was an abusive man, Mama had taken all of her children and left him. I don't know what she said to him, but she got him to drive her and all six children to her mother's home. She stayed there until she was able to get her own place.

As an adult, I can see that Lilly, by the grace of God, got herself out of an abusive relationship. I didn't see the abuse happening. But I realize there were physical vestiges of it left over. Being a Mama's Girl, I would sit and oil her scalp and comb her hair. That's when I would see the scars in her head from where she'd told me that he'd beaten her with a high-heeled shoe. I was very young and I don't recall any of that. Yet, I had no reason not to believe her, especially with me seeing the scars on her scalp with my own eyes. Those were physical scars. I have no idea what other scars she carried, but even this knowledge helps in seeing her as a full person. I'm not the only one who has experienced pain. This understanding makes it easier to forgive.

We were living in another city and several years went by. One day Mama came home with this tall man. She introduced him as our new dad. They had gotten married and we were moving to another town.

We all moved together and settled into our new home as a family. My mother was the disciplinarian and handled all of the corporal punishment. My father went to work and came home. He was a good man, a quiet man, and he was nice to me. I didn't know much but I knew that she took good care of him. She cooked all of his meals and served him first. There were times that she would instruct me to make him a chess pie because he liked them. I regret to say that as a teenager, I didn't always want to cook them and at times I had a bad attitude. One day I was mad because I had to make them and I really didn't care how they turned out so it was not my best. Is this not how we act with God? He loves us and takes care of our needs and we get an attitude when He asks us to do a thing that's inconvenient?!

When I would reminisce years later I would feel bad because he was the only father that I had known and I wouldn't want to do something as simple as cooking the pies for him. This man took care of six children that were not his own biological children. That's some type of love in action right there! I would correct people when they would refer to him as my stepfather. I'd quickly respond, "No, he's my father." He used to give me a silver half dollar for my birthday. After a couple of years, Mama stopped him from doing that because "if you do it for one, you have to do it for all of them." That bothered me because we didn't normally get cakes or a birthday party. That was the only special thing that was done for me on my birthday. I was bummed that I didn't get the half dollars anymore either. But that's just the way it was.

Truth be told, I felt special because my father saw me and took an opportunity to acknowledge me, the one who got lost in the sauce. Looking back, I can see that this is how God saw me; worthy of being recognized and acknowledged on my birthday, for simply being created; for simply being Rhonda. I realize I may have been Mama's Girl, but I was always Abba's Pearl according to Matthew 13:45-46, sought out and of great value.

I noticed that my father had begun to lose weight, and had lost a significant amount of weight within a six-to-nine month period of time. He didn't go to the doctor much and the only reason that he went was because he started seeing blood in his urine. The surgeon looked in his belly with a laparoscope and found cancer throughout his body. In less than three months, he was gone. This was very hard for me. He was my Daddy regardless of the genes and he loved me. I'm sure it was hard for my mother, as well. They had been married for fourteen or fifteen years when he died. I can't imagine what she felt.

Mama not only took care of him, she took care of us, too. She raised us. There is a difference between having children and raising them. And to be quite honest, she did most of it as a single parent. We played the game of Scrabble a lot as a family and we would show each other our letters to help each other out with our words. We had fun and for the most part we were not that serious about the competitive aspect of it. It was about spending time together and enjoying each other's company. She would give us spelling tests and call out one hundred words for us to spell. As I mentioned earlier, she valued education so much. Education was not only school-related. Mama taught me how to do everything. I learned to wash the dishes, how to chop wood, mow the grass, cook, clean and take care of myself. We all did. The boys knew how to wash clothes and clean, too. Even as adult men they know how to cook a turkey dinner or whatever from scratch. She was a visionary with wisdom. She prepared us to be self-sufficient as she had been. She was also an old school disciplinarian. She believed in the biblical passage, "Spare the rod and spoil the child." One of her famous quotes was, "Drop them drawers, I don't whoop no clothes." And if anyone is wondering, yes, we got beat with switches and even extension cords. However, she didn't slap us in the face. "God provided a better place," she'd say before we got disciplined. The better place she was talking about was our backside!

Mama had a heart to help people she felt needed assistance. She would gather hand-me-downs from our home as well as other families that she knew and donate them to a big family known to us. I remember, even as a child, thinking that you don't step on people in your house to help people on the outside. Subconsciously, I felt that she often treated strangers better than she treated me, her own daughter. I can and do only speak from my own experiences. I was soon to learn through a forthcoming diagnosis that this still proved to be a true assessment of how differently I was treated.

We did have love but my mother wasn't one to say I love you. Still I knew that she did love me. Sometimes people need more than just being left to assume that they are loved. They need the demonstration of that love in more ways than one. Sometimes, I, Rhonda, needed more than my own reassurance that I was loved. I needed the verbalization and demonstration of that love in more ways than one. I didn't really have the words for it then, but I needed to know I had value. I needed to know I was not a throwaway or an afterthought or one to be tolerated or lost.

I shared a few of these snippets from my mother's

life to show who and how she was and to introduce the mixed feelings that I ascribe to my relationship with her. It was simultaneously simple and complex like a lot of human relationships. She had deep things to deal with as a woman: loss of confidence in pursuing her education, an abusive marriage, the death of two husbands; one of whom was abusive, one of whom was kind, and six children which did not seem like a burden, but how would I know what she thought about when she laid down at night?

As I said, Mama was more than a mother. My mother, Lilly, was also a daughter with a complex mother-daughter relationship of her own. Earlier I mentioned the confession that rocked my sixteen-year-old world: Mama had to learn to love her mother so she could learn to love me. I believe this was the key to unraveling why my mother behaved as she did towards me though she declared her feelings had changed.

❧ Lilly's Mama ❧

I MAY HAVE NEVER PUT THESE THINGS together except that when I started on this writing journey, I remembered Mama's confession. Was the schism in their relationship the reason why I sat under the kitchen table in distress? What actually happened between them that caused them to have problems in their relationship? These wounds were still so deep that when Grandmama died, I did not see my mother cry. What was it that happened in my grandmother's life that had such a significant impact that she passed it down to my mother and was to have been passed down to me and to my daughter?

Mama and Grandma, who we also called Grandmama, interacted with one another but it was not a warm relationship from what I witnessed. My family lived fairly close to my grandmother. So even though one of her sons lived on the property next door to her, my mother took on the role of chauffeur whenever Grandma needed to go

to "town." Grandmama was half-blind but fiercely independent. That independent gene runs deep and wide in
this family bloodline. Mama would load us into the tan
station wagon and we would pick Grandma up from her
farm. Then we would drive her either around town or to
the next town so that she could take care of her own le-
gal business, grocery shop, and wash her clothes at the
laundromat. They would sit in the front seat of the car and
talk while the children were in the back. When we brought
Grandma back home, we unloaded her stuff from the car
and departed. I now understand that this was Mama's
way of "honoring" her mother. For reasons that only she
knew, she felt that it was her responsibility to transport
Grandma so that she could carry out her affairs. It may
have been because at this time she was the daughter that
lived closest to her mother.

I feel led to tell you that my grandmother was very
respected in the community. She was an astute business-
woman and in Mama's words, "She knew how to make
money!" She owned lots of property and her name carried
a lot of weight around the city. After she completed her list
of things to do, we would take her back home. We never,
ever ate at her place because, to be honest, there was no
running water. In addition, the kitchen wasn't used as a
kitchen. It was just another room full of stuff. She had an
outhouse, not a functional inside bathroom. There was
stuff piled everywhere and she had very little living space
due to massive clutter piled in most of the rooms. Two

or three of her houses had burned to the ground due to her wood burning stoves and clutter. Somehow, even with Grandmama's poor living conditions she began to take care of three of her great-grandchildren. My mother did not agree with this. All I know is one day we went to the farm and when we left those three children came home with us. It was not a pretty transaction. There was a tug-of-war, some pulling and I saw Grandma's mouth opened as if to bite Mama. I had never seen my mother or grand-mother respond like this before. Mama was determined to bring those children home with her. They stayed with us for a while and then they went somewhere else, but not back to my grandmother's place. Looking back on it, there was a battle for control happening before my eyes. Which of them was right? I don't know. But neither was giving up without a fight.

This was even more puzzling to me when Mama told me that when she was a little girl, Grandmama would take her everywhere that she went. She did this because to leave her at home would mean Mama would be left with her siblings and mistreated. As she said, "I was sand-wiched between two mean ones." Again, I am plagued with the question of what wounds were obviously deep-seated and raw enough to cause Mama's love to be on hold for me until she could amend their relationship?

Because, Grandmama sheltered Mama from her siblings, I believe Mama raised us in a peaceful environ-ment meaning there was not a lot of outside drama entering our home nor was there excessive drama inside the home. Mama ruled the house with an iron fist; what she said goes, period, end of discussion. We did not have a contentious household. There was also not a lot of discussion regarding what you were told to do and the expectation that it would be done in a timely manner. There was an overall atmosphere of peace within the home.

I have learned that I also create an atmosphere of peace within my own home. Similarly, we are very protective of our children from outside danger. But what happened in the between years that caused the division between mother and daughter? What rift was so big that Mama couldn't look at her own baby daughter because she looked so much like her mother?

A few years later something happened. I was still living at home and I was working part-time and taking full-time classes at the local college. One day I was startled awake to see Mama standing beside the bed. I jumped when I saw her and she said, "Come get the car. I wrecked it." I was confused.

"What?"

"I was driving to Mona's house and I hit a car at the intersection. Come get it."

The end result was that she was driving to a friend's house when she hit a TransAm at the intersection. I never got the full story of what actually happened but that fancy car was totaled while her station wagon only had a little dent. From that day on, she never drove another car. When she was asked, she would just say my nerves are too bad. Now because Mama had stopped driving, she now depended upon her children, mostly me, to take her wherever she wanted to go.

After that incident, I would pick up Grandmama and take her to conduct her business. I don't recall how many times that I did this. On the ride, she would talk about working on the farm and other random things. Oddly enough we did not talk about any of her children, my mother included. Our topics varied, but one day, I asked my grandmother about my Granddaddy.

"I don't know anything about him. What kind of man was he? He was dead before I was born and you never talk about him" I said.

"The best thing he ever did for me was to die," she said. I was shocked when that came out of her mouth. I was not expecting that at all. That was all she would say. As was her intent, I didn't ask Grandmama any more questions about Grandaddy. I did learn later that he was a preacher. He died when Mama was eighteen. I learned he had beat Mama with a tobacco stick. I always wondered what would make this preacher beat his daughter. And was that what made her leave home? Or was the beating a result of her informing him that she was leaving? Was he always abusive? Or just that day? Was this why Mama didn't love Grandmama? Because she didn't feel protected from Granddaddy? Why didn't any of the aunts or uncles talk about their earlier years at home? There was so much secrecy and quiet around their lives. There were so many questions, and yet so few answers about the real history of this family.

When Grandmama died, my mother, who I lived with at the time, did not shed a single tear. Well, not that I saw. What was even more strange was this: according to Mama, Grandmama had asked her to speak at her home-going celebration. I still don't understand their relationship or what happened between them. There are so many things that seemed to have occurred and frankly I was probably just too young to remember.

What I do know is that Mom stopped some things she saw in her own house growing up. I don't know the complete story, but there are skeletons in the closet concerning men watching the children. Mama was very particular about who she allowed to watch her children. She made it known on several occasions that men could not be trusted around young children. We were not allowed to go visit other children or spend the night. She was adamant about it. I didn't know it, but I was determined to do the same in protecting my daughter. My mother offered me protection from the outside world. But not from her.

Why do I say that? The source of my greatest pain has been rejection from my mother. I had unmet needs from my mother, namely the need for acceptance and approval. Left unrecognized and unchecked, it would create dysfunction. Had the Holy Spirit not revealed that, I would have then passed that dysfunction down to my daughter and my daughter would carry that cycle of unmet needs and dysfunction down the bloodline. But God. I am a chain breaker. Generational curses stop with me. The same cycles and patterns of behaviors would not plague my daughter or her children. Generational blessings, however, will continue in my lifetime and be passed down to my daughter and her children and children's children to come.

❧ How I Broke the Chains ☙

"When I focused on God, the results were even more profound. God loved me. He loved me unconditionally."

- Rhonda

❧ Chain Breakers ❧

Recognizing My Need

WHEN YOU'RE A "YES MAMA" GIRL, it's easy to be manipulated and persuaded to do things that you really don't want to do. You just go along to get along. I didn't want any trouble, I just wanted to be loved. I wanted to be seen as valuable in my mother's eyes. And the thing is, I didn't know that was what I wanted. I surely didn't know it's what I needed. What I didn't realize is that God answered that need. The more I filled up on the Word and heeded the voice of the Holy Spirit, the less I needed Mama to validate me. When I think about it, Mama got all of my attention and devotion because there was no one else to really shower me with it nor was there anyone in my life to compete for it. Once I began seeing someone that rapidly changed. When I focused on God, the results were even more profound. God loved me. He loved me unconditionally. I stated in an earlier section that I could confidently parent my daughter. That confidence was not inherent to me. I mentioned that I had low self-esteem and felt I was unattractive. For someone who experiences these feelings, the confidence is also pretty low in most areas. But I needed that confidence. And God began to instill it in me. He filled me up. The refueling came from rededicating my life to Him and I saw it in my ability to care for my daughter. From my father, I now understand that like God, he saw me. He did that one simple thing on my birthdays to make me feel special; like I had value. The value of his actions didn't come from the silver half dollar that he gave me. It was the act of giving me the silver half dollar. I just thought it was the rejection that I didn't want. I didn't know until I began this writing process that I needed to feel special in someone's eyes. Jesus left the ninety nine to track down the one who'd wandered away. I was once the one sheep who got lost. I needed to be found. Jesus did that for me.

JOURNAL PROMPT: Can you think of any unmet needs that you have experienced with your mother? Take some time now to write them out using the provided space. While this book is about my mother and a portion of our relationship, your unmet needs could stem from a relationship with a father or another important person in your life. Once you have written these out, is there a specific unmet need that is causing you not to walk in your purpose? Is there one that is demanding your attention?

_____

_____

_____

_____

_____

_____

_____

_____

_____

_____

Saying No

Saying no to my mother in those early days was the beginning of me changing the trajectory of my life. (Hint: It will work for you, too.) It was the start of breaking a spirit of dysfunction and generational curse off the mother-daughter relationships in my family, well, at least for my daughter and me. It must be noted that we, as people, often imitate what we see and are influenced by what we are around. Either we will repeat the behaviors, or we will go in another direction and not follow the same path. Let me reiterate that it was the very beginning of the change in our relationship. There was a long road ahead of us. Some of the roads had detours and side roads that developed and needed to be navigated through. If I have one regret, it would be that I didn't start saying no sooner. "No" is a powerful tool to stop a controlling and manipulative person in their tracks. Will they try other tactics? Most likely. But saying no is the beginning of breaking patterns and cycles despite the need for love.

🖊 JOURNAL PROMPT: *What are some things going on in your life that you know without a doubt that you need to start saying no to?*

_____

_____

_____

_____

_____

_____

_____

Identifying Patterns

A pattern is described by Merriam-Webster as a "reliable sample of traits, acts, tendencies, or other observable characteristics of a person, group or institution." In other words, it's an example for others to follow. These patterns obviously can be positive or negative, and the impact of either one can draw a family together, or divide and damage it completely.

There are definitely patterns of behavior that I saw in both my grandmother and my mother. They were overall very quiet women in nature but they both got exactly what they wanted when they wanted it. Both were very respected and both ruled their households with a strong will. I didn't grow up in my grandmother's household so I can only speak about what I saw when we visited her. She handled her business with authority and was well respected for her business acumen. There was one thing about my grandmother that was confusing to me. How did someone who had such control over her business affairs have a home that was in such extreme disarray? In that way there was a stark difference between her and Mama. In any case, stubbornness and strong will were very much in action in both. Could a reason for their clashing be because they were very much like one another, unwilling to bend or to compromise or to address the pain in their lives? I'd noticed that when I confronted my mother about a certain behavior, she did not respond. When I asked Grandma about Granddaddy she shut that down with a quickness. Is this how they operated?

I didn't know that I had a controlling mother who may have had a controlling mother until I became a whole adult. When you are born into something and you have no reference point, you just don't know any better. It's almost like being subconsciously groomed to agree with whatever that person wants or even says without acknowledging your own voice or opinion. I just thought of Mama as being "harsh" and very strong willed. I learned that I could honor her by doing what she asked. But there needed to be some boundaries set which involved saying no.

🖊 JOURNAL PROMPT: *As you read this section, have you identified patterns of behavior that you didn't recognize previously? Write them down.*

_____

_____

_____

_____

_____

_____

_____

_____

_____

_____

_____

_____

Changing My Thought Process

Several years after my daughter was born I began attending a church where the Pastor taught us how God desires a personal relationship with us. He taught about a transformation that God wanted to do in us. As a matter of fact, he was the first true "Pastor" that I felt I had ever had. He taught the Bible. He taught us what God expected of us and I was blown away. Even though I had been in church all of my life, initially, I felt like a new babe in Christ under his leadership. It was because this teaching was an awakening to me and the trajectory of my life took another turn. I was more aware of the Holy Spirit leading, guiding, and directing me and the pull of Mama was losing momentum. I really felt a change inside of me. Did I make the right decision every time? No, I didn't. But there was a change in my thought process and how I looked at my relationship with my mother. Earlier in the book, I recalled a phone conversation in which Mama was telling me something specific that I should do. "You're not in control of my life," I said. "Holy Spirit is in control of what I do." I knew that the power of the Holy Spirit was guiding me and giving me the strength to break free from someone who used love as an instrument or even a weapon to control and manipulate. I know this sounds brutal, but the truth sometimes can be. I continued to honor and respect my mother, but the bands of control were beginning to loosen their tight hold.

The initial changes of my thought process involved allowing the Holy Spirit to reign. The Holy Spirit helps with decision-making and gives revelation to aid us in the thought process. The Holy Spirit teaches us about the inherent love that God has towards us and how to exhibit it to others.

The spirit of rejection takes on many forms and if we're not observant, it will mask itself as something else. We can be set free and healed from rejection. However, as part of changing one's thought process, we first must recognize and acknowledge that the spirit of rejection is real and we are held hostage by it. I know of several people who are in acute denial that they are dealing with a spirit of rejection. When rejection is present and not dealt with, it brings other spirits of anger, rage, abandonment, the orphan spirit, and offense just to name a few. I just did not understand what was wrong with me that my mother responded to me the way that she did. And why did it manifest whenever there was an audience to witness it? In certain moments where those spirits attached to rejection would arise, I would have that same quick vision of me sitting under the table crying and pulling my hair. The details are missing about what transpired that day, but I know for a fact that rejection was present and if it is not dealt with, it can be passed down to the next generation, destroying relationships in its wake.

As previously mentioned, I did not understand what a spirit of rejection was until I became an adult. Years later I began attending an Apostolic-Prophetic Church. It was there that I began to grow leaps and bounds spiritually. I was now seeing Rhonda, not in relation to Mama or siblings as I did as a child of four years old, or even as a teenager, but in relation to God and my relationship with Him. I knew that Mama treated me differently from the other siblings, and they knew it as well. I recognized that in families, sometimes we are torn. We feel bad for the person going through it, but at the same time, we are thankful that we are not in the same position they are in. And we keep it moving.

✏ JOURNAL PROMPT: *Are there some thought processes that may be keeping you held captive? Thoughts of defeat, anguish or hopelessness? You don't have to hold onto them any longer. Just lay them down and allow Jesus to renew your mind and redirect your thought pattern.*

_____

_____

_____

_____

_____

_____

_____

_____

_____

_____

_____

_____

Deliverance

To be delivered is to be rescued by God. In the Psalms, David constantly asks God to deliver him. Sometimes we need deliverance or rescue from our enemies and/or that which plagues us and chases us down. I will talk more deeply about the actual act of deliverance in a later chapter. But not only was God delivering me from rejection, He was delivering me from the spirit of religion. The spirit of religion shows up in our services that are so programmed that there is no room for the Holy Spirit to move. So to be delivered from religion was to allow the Holy Spirit to have a say so in my life; to be able to speak. But rejection still had to be dealt with. As a child, I didn't *feel* like I was rejected. Better yet, I did not have language for the things happening to me or how my heart received those unnamed arrows. Mama raised us all with the same iron fist. She was a firm believer in discipline. I was just living my life as a daughter, a sister, a friend, a student, all of my many different roles. I knew there was a difference but I could not pinpoint why there was a difference. It kept me questioning if there was something wrong with me.

I would say that the spirit of rejection consistently became apparent after I became a young adult. There were little things here and there but nothing so blatant that it shined like a beacon. Yes, I recall seeing me under the table as a toddler, but after that, no other incidents came to mind until that fateful day when Mama told me about not loving her mother when I was born. I do know that I have felt less than the others in my family. The teenage version of Rhonda had always felt insecure and shy; very unsure of herself and unvalued. I only had one or two friends in middle school and during high school years, I really didn't have any friends at all. I talked to people at school but rarely out of a school environment. We didn't participate in any extracurricular activities because there were six children in the family. Mama had always said, "If I can't do it for all, then I won't do it for one." She told us often that there were too many of us to try and join different organizations and groups. "I wouldn't be able to haul everyone around." Because of that, we didn't participate in anything. And because Mama didn't believe in us spending the night with other people, we all stayed at home.

Even though Mama had divulged her feelings about learning to love her mother and me, I didn't see blatant rejection. Or maybe I just didn't recognize it for what it was. It was only when I had reached my mid-twenties and had moved out that it truly became clear to me. These were the days that she rejected my gifts and would poke at me when others came around.

I suppose I had been an easy target because initially I didn't process what it really was. Looking back at my younger years, the manipulation was probably an early indication of Mama's attitude towards me. I was an obedient child. I did what I was told to do. Some might even call it brain washing or some form of emotional abuse. Naivete, the desire to please, and a desire to be loved was the open door for manipulation and control. The spirit of rejection presented itself at my birth and began to weave its web from that point, literally laying low until it was revealed.

It's difficult to remember all of the antagonistic comments that have been made throughout a lifetime of interactions with Mama. I am grateful for the inability to remember those things or hold a grudge or else I could truly have become a bitter, angry, and hateful person.

Unless one is completely numb to it or delivered, rejection in any shape, form, or fashion is painful. And when abandonment that came in the form of people I thought were my friends is added in the mix, it can be un-bearable. I believe timing is so important. When a person is abandoned in one of the most vulnerable times in their life, the effects can take a lifetime to overcome. Imagine how many women have made poor choices only to be left carrying the bag or baby by themselves. And it is no differ-ent than when men are abandoned by their counterparts and left to raise children without the assistance of a wife or mother to the children. When Isaac was completely out of the picture, there was hurt and there was pain. Some of it stemmed from the fact that I let my guard down long enough to be deceived. I believed that he would be there for the baby as he said he would. I believed that everything was going to be alright. And it was, just not with him.

🖉 JOURNAL PROMPT: *Sometimes it is hard for us to let*

go of some of these things and we need help. Some of you may not be familiar with the ministry of deliverance and that is okay. If you are led to, search out deliverance ministries and connect with the one that you feel can meet your needs.

———————————————————————

———————————————————————

———————————————————————

———————————————————————

Letting Go of Unmet Expectations

When I let all of the unrealistic, unmet expectations go, I was firmly on my road to deliverance from the chains that held me captive and freedom. My expectation of Isaac was released. My expectation of my mother's acceptance was released. She loved me the way she could. And I was responsible for the boundaries and safeguards for my heart. To refuse to let go of my expectations would be to open myself up to continued disappointment and bitterness. God had so much more for me to focus on. I was not going to settle for less than God's best for me any longer. Once this decision was made, it impacted all of my relationships. I was not going to settle for one-sided relationships where I was the only one reaching out, calling and initiating conversations or whatever. I now know that I was in a process of separation. The Creator was calling me to come out from what I had previously valued as important into a deeper relationship with Him. I had value as a person, as a daughter, as a sister, as an employee, as a friend, and yes, as a mother. I had value for simply being created by God in His image; for simply being Rhonda. I was loved just because. I am loved just because.

🖊 JOURNAL PROMPT: *All of us have value and we are loved by God. At this time I would ask you to journal as many valuable attributes as you can think of. Your personality, your smile, your caring nature, your sense of humor, your wealth of knowledge, etc. The list can go on and on. After you write this list, just look at it and know that you are of great value; to God first of all, and then to the people that you are called in impact and influence.*

Overcoming

The first step in overcoming anything is to first recognize what is actually happening. What exactly is the issue? What is really going on? I was able to unearth a pattern of discord between my mother and grandmother. I was able to recognize my need, regain strength by saying no, and change my thought process. I have let go of unmet expectations. I have identified the spirit of rejection. Getting to the root of rejection would be nice but at this point I don't know that I ever will know the root unless the Holy Spirit reveals it to me.

However, I do know this: Everything that happened was designed to make me despise God; to run from Him instead of toward Him, to blame Him instead of seek Him; to seek approval from human beings instead of relationship with God. Can you imagine the shame the church would have heaped on me had I confessed in front of them? Relationship with God gave me the strength to stand up against the spirit of rejection. God taught me to reject religiosity for a relationship with Him. He taught me how to not let others' opinion of me take away from who He called me to be. God taught me to seek Him for guidance; to assert myself with confidence that His wisdom is enough. God does not waste anything that He allows us to go through. I cried so many tears for many years from hurt with no real answers as to why the hurt existed. The person who is supposed to love me the most was the one who was causing me the most pain. But God stepped in.

🖊 JOURNAL PROMPT: *Take time to think about a situation you may have gone through. Assess your life now that you are on the other side. What are some steps that you took in order to overcome them? How can you apply them to your current situation?*

_____

_____

_____

_____

_____

_____

_____

_____

Forgiveness

Last, but not least, there is no overcoming without forgiveness. I'm talking about forgiving the person and they don't even acknowledge that they have wronged you. I couldn't forgive without having love in my heart and I couldn't have love in my heart without Jesus. He loves me and forgives me for all of the mess ups that I have had. I could not forgive without Him. The love of God overpowered all of the pain, hurt, bitterness, and the walls that I had built up in my heart. When Jesus's love moved in, all of that other junk had to exit the premises.

I began to pray and to repent for allowing those feelings that were not of God to control my actions and behaviors. Because of the rejection that I was experiencing, I had begun to let it contaminate my spirit and I was not showing or exhibiting the love that I professed was inside of me. I asked God to remove the hurt, remove the pain, remove the wall of hardness that was there. I also asked God to help me to let go of the past and to not allow it to hinder my future relationships with my spouse, my children, or anyone that I had a relationship with. I had asked God to remove all of those things and I had to be willing to release them to Him. In releasing all of the trauma, I gained peace of mind and I also gained a newfound determination to break the cycle, to break the generational curse of mother-daughter dysfunction. What my Mama saw in me reminded her of her mother and whatever unresolved trauma that she had experienced. My daughter would not share the same story.

One of the first feelings that I encountered was anguish and then remorse. I felt the anguish because I allowed bitterness to enter my heart. That is not one of the fruit of the spirit. Bitterness is a work of the flesh and when it came in it brought some of its friends with it. I became resentful and soon anger towards my mother set in. I was so hurt and disappointed. Those were the days that I stopped calling her Mama and started addressing her as Lilly. It was my way of detaching myself from the pain of the interactions with her.

Freedom came in gradual increments. The stronger that I became spiritually, the less control the enemy had over my emotions. As I gained knowledge through an intentional seeking of God, I began to heal. When old ways tried to resurface, I was in a better mental and emotional state and able to combat the fiery darts that would come my way. And things did get better between me and Mama. At least they did on my end. She enjoyed maintaining her independence within her own home and she welcomed daily, weekly, and for some, just monthly visits from her children and grandchildren. But nothing comes easy. There was another season blowing into town.

✎JOURNAL PROMPT: *Forgiveness is such an important step in our healing process. But not just forgiving the other person or persons. We must actively engage and forgive ourselves. Releasing ourselves from the bondage of unforgiveness is just as vital as forgiving others. Can you think someone in your life that you need to forgive? Can you think of something that may have happened in the past or even recently for which you need to forgive yourself and allow yourself to be healed?*

Rhonda Joyce

_____

_____

_____

_____

_____

_____

_____

_____

_____

_____

ȣ   Plot Twist   Ȥ

I HAD BEGUN TO NOTICE that there were occasions in which Mama would forget things. To be honest, we all do it to a certain extent. This though, was not the usual forgetting of things. Then she began to repeat the same things over and over and over again. All of her children recognized it. On occasion, we mentioned it to one another to see if one was experiencing the same thing with her as the other. She still functioned as normal for the most part, but it became a running joke to count how many times Mom would ask the same question or repeat things when we would visit her. What I now know is that these were the initial moments that we began to recognize that a cognitive change had taken place in Mama.

A big clue for me was the fact that although Mama and I talked just about every morning, there were subtle changes in our conversations that I began to notice more and more. We most certainly had reached a stage where most of the time there was peace and harmony between us. I had grown so much spiritually that I was no longer hesitant about expressing how something that she had said bothered me. During this season I had begun walking most mornings between six and six-thirty. I would call and talk to her while I was walking. It helped the time go by faster and distracted me from thinking about how much I didn't want to be out there walking. Plus for as long as I can remember, Mama has gotten up with the chickens! She was usually awake by four in the morning, had her clothes on, and had eaten breakfast by five or six o'clock. When I was working, I would also call her or she would call me on my way to work every morning during my 30-40 minute commute. We would also converse periodically throughout the day.

One day I noticed that Mama was not calling me like she used to. I would call her and she would say, "I was thinking about you, but was too lazy to pick up the phone." This actually went on for some months. She would call occasionally but for the most part, her phone calls to me gradually stopped. When we did talk, there was that repetition of words that I mentioned earlier.

Another major behavior change that was noted was that Mama was constantly "looking for the kids." We found out later that she was not sleeping because was up and down all night looking throughout the house for these kids. The phone would ring and Mama would be on the other end asking how many children were at her house because they were gone. Also, she was always ready to "go home" and would actually try to leave her own house to head "home." The end result would be Mama leaving from the house around midnight one October morning. The police found her the next morning. After an examination at the local emergency room, she was discharged home where we began to stay with her 24 hours a day, seven days a week. Whoever was available and would help was enlisted; children, grandchildren, friends, and even in-laws helped to ensure that Mama was not left alone.

We were given an unofficial diagnosis of dementia by her physician based on his observation of her during a doctor's visit combined with our report of her recent actions and behaviors. Even though mama's cognitive functions had changed, her independence and strong will had not! Caring for an independent, strong willed mother with dementia is not a task for the faint of heart! This presented a whole other set of challenges and opportunities. But that's for a later date.

But that's not the true plot twist.

Mama's dementia brought back old patterns of behavior and old ways that were not very pleasant towards me. And to be completely honest, it happened regularly. It really is hard to explain. The disregard and dismissal of anything that I had to say was back. Oh yes, the extra smart remarks and attitude returned with a vengeance, only this time it wasn't just me that it was aimed at. She exhibited these same mannerisms towards my daughter who'd agreed to sit with Mama in the evening. Even though her mind came and went, it amazed me as to how selective she still was. Different people were saying that they, as in dementia patients, don't know what they're doing, but it remained to be seen as far as I was concerned.

Years before Allie was born, Mama had gotten sick and was admitted to the local hospital. Several of us came to the hospital to visit as she was placed in her room. While we were all together, Mama's doctor came in to speak with her. She turned to me and one other person and said, "Rhonda, you and Janice need to leave the room."

I had a memory of Mama's reaction when I got my first Nursing degree. Her exact words were, "Don't be trying to diagnose me." I responded with laughter saying, "Mama, no one is going to try to diagnose you."

I laughed, but apparently she was serious. Mama was very specific about who she wanted to know her business. I now realize the magnitude of her order. I had no authority to call her doctor and request medications at her design. She made sure that my name was not on any of her medical records. That was not an issue until later in Mama's life. I was still getting calls from Mama saying, "Call the doctor's office for me." She would ask me to request a refill of her medication. Of course, when I called they politely refused to give me any information. After another request to contact her doctor for a refill was denied, I told Mama not to call me again about her medical history or medication. Unless I was added to the list, it didn't make sense for her to continue to ask me to do these things for her.

Mama was doing her best to keep me out of the loop. I didn't think it was a matter of trust. She asked me to take her everywhere and if she didn't feel like going, she trusted me to shop for her. As I said, I was low on the food chain. Fortunately, I was also much stronger to deal with her shenanigans on a mental level. But now that dementia was present, those old patterns of behavior have come back with a vengeance.

With the return of this behavior, I am now convinced that there's an unpredictable and blatant rejection of my voice, ideas, or maybe just me as a person. To add insult to injury, the same disregard that she has for me, seemed to have migrated to my daughter, only worse. Allie would stay with her during the evening because we wanted to have someone be with her. After a few months, Allie decided she'd had enough.

"For my mental health, I'm not doing this." Allie had done nothing to her, but Mama was displaying a smart attitude towards her and anything that she said. Now mind you Mama kept Allie for the first four years of her life while I worked. In fact, the first words that she uttered were "Granny's juice." She would also stay with "Granny" when I had to work on the weekends or to go out of town. Mama would also keep her during the summer months while school was out. Allie had a very good relationship with Mama, and Mama had never talked ugly to Allie. This was new and very hurtful to my daughter. As far as we could see, Mama seemed to be very selective in how she spoke to different people. Allie and I bore the brunt of her rude behavior. People would say, "Don't take it personal. She doesn't know what she's doing." I can agree with that to a certain extent, but I remember thinking, "If you don't know what you're doing, then why don't you treat everyone the same way?"

So maybe I was right. Saying no to her agitated her. Or maybe it was that there was something in her that was agitated by what and Who was in me. All I knew was that the old behaviors were back; rejection was back. I think the root of her rejection of me has everything to do with her mother and is solely directed at me and my daughter. I thought I was delivered. There is an old saying, "No test, no testimony!"

This was the test. Had I forgiven? Had I truly overcome?

❧ How I Overcame ❧

"And they overcame him by the blood of the Lamb, and by the word of their testimony; and they loved not their lives unto the death."

- Revelation 12:11

⮾ Overcoming: A New Testimony ⮿

A VITAL PART OF OVERCOMING is our testimony. A testimony tells the story of an adverse situation or condition, and then continues with how you came out of it. Revelation 12:11 states, *"And they overcame him by the blood of the Lamb, and by the word of their testimony; and they loved not their lives unto the death."* What does it mean to overcome? The Greek definition of overcome or *nikao* means to conquer or carry the victory of Christ. Who did we overcome? The accuser of the brethren. That's Satan or the Devil. Simply put, the blood of the Lamb is Jesus's blood that was shed on the cross. Testimony or *martyria* is a testifying or one who testifies before a judge. So we conquer the accuser through Jesus and our testifying before God. It sounds so simple, but our faith in Jesus and testimony can help us to overcome the arrows that Satan launches our way. The testimony is not the only thing that helps us but there is a huge role that our testimony plays.

First, it helps us to name the trouble we've faced. Secondly, it gives honor to the God who helped us come through the trouble. His power is, thus, glorified. Sharing our story and how God brought us through pain and adversity can in turn help someone who is going through the same or similar situation. It can't be dismissed as irrelevant or insignificant. What would be my testimony? Would I overcome this renewed hurdle?

Overcoming: New Life

Several years ago, I had a conversation with a leader and conveyed that I felt that there was "more" to God than what I had been experiencing. Someone told me about this pastor who I began to research on YouTube. Turns out, he was going to be at a revival near my hometown.

One evening in July 2018, I went to the tent revival. On this night, the Holy Spirit prompted me to go to the front for prayer. I had never in my life been personally prayed over like that. The Pastor called out issues that I had been having. Nobody there knew anything about them because they didn't know me like that. I had been going to a Baptist Church for most of my adult life. But right there in that moment, I knew something was happening that I had never experienced before. Through that word of knowledge, I am reminded yet again that God knew me by name. He had given a revelation to the prophet about me!

I ended up going to the revival every single night

that it was there. The "more" that I sensed was missing from my God experience was happening in that place. This was a side of God that I had never felt before and I loved what I was feeling.

I knew I wasn't released to leave my current church yet. I had recently shared with my Leader that the LORD had "called" me to be an Evangelist. He accepted my calling and I was given instructions as a minister-in-training. I continued my other ministry duties as I sat under leadership for training. I would go to service in the morning to fulfill my responsibilities as a member, and then leave to drive to the Apostolic/Pentecostal church to catch the rest of their service. I had already been commissioned by the LORD to preach the Gospel but I didn't understand why I felt pulled to this House of Worship.

Each week that I came, I would sit in the back row. I did this mainly because the church would be full and only the ushers' seats would be empty. There was such an anointing on the service and people were being delivered from unclean spirits, miraculous healings were taking place, and prophetic utterances were going forth. It was unlike anything that I had ever experienced before in my life. Even if I only got the last 30 minutes it was everything that I needed for the week. I was also still trying to figure out what it was that kept me coming back to this church over and over again.

One Sunday, the Pastor called me up from the back row to the altar. He began to speak healing over me and to prophesy concerning my daughter and me. I ended up passed out on the floor! There was new life for me at New Life. I knew God was calling me there. One day months later, I went to the altar for prayer and the intercessor said, "I don't know what this means but I heard the LORD say, "It's time." I was questioning what that meant because I knew it was something big. I had also been seeking the LORD for a specific answer concerning when it was time for me to transition from my current church. I knew that God was drawing me closer and revealing more of Himself to me. I had to make a decision that would change my life forever. Spiritual well-being is just as important, if not, more important than our physical well-being.

The actual act of leaving my current church was hard because twenty years is a long time. Relationships were built and cultivated in those twenty years. But one thing stood firm: my time was up. I was intent on becoming who God created Rhonda to be. My new life was ahead of me.

I have learned throughout my lifetime that freedom from any kind of unclean spirit or oppression can only be found in the love of the Father. John 8:36 states, *"If the Son therefore shall make you free, ye shall be free indeed."* This spirit of rejection that had plagued my life thus far was not going to keep me bound, sad, and longing any longer. When I received the full freedom that the Father gave me through His Son, Jesus, the walk out of that took on a whole new meaning. God's love transcends us and causes us to go higher in the things of the Spirit, which causes the works of the flesh to take a back seat in our lives.

As I've mentioned before, strength from God elevates us to a position where the enemy's power no longer has control over us. The love of my heavenly Father strengthened me in such a way that the stronghold was cast down and its power was crushed under my feet. It was there the entire time, I was just not in a place to receive it and believe it.

Overcoming: Recognizing the Power of God's Love

God's love revealed to me that there was nothing wrong with me. I was exactly who He created me to be and if that wasn't enough, then they (whoever they may be) needed to take that up with Him. I may have not been enough for a mother's unconditional love, but I was certainly enough for the Father's love, for Abba's love.

Walking through this process has been one of the most painful things that I have ever had to go through in my life. But I take hope in the fact that there is purpose in my pain. My healing is found only in relationship with Jesus. His love destroys the other stuff that is contrary to His will for me. I Peter 4:8 says, *"Most important of all, continue to show deep love for each other, for love covers a multitude of sins."* Love covers a multitude of sins, and when the love of Jesus is in your heart, there is really no other option but to love and forgive. This love is not something that you can conjure up. It must come from God because God is love and love in itself is spiritual. It is not carnal or fleshy. This love is so powerful and pure that it caused me to be unable to hold any animosity or hatred towards the one person who hurt me the most. I had to think about how I love my family and how that love won't let me mistreat them. As powerful as that love is, I had to think about God's love for me. He loved me so much that according to John 3:16, He sent His only Son to die for me so that I could live with Him in eternity. The love of God humbles me and causes me to strive even more to let Him know that I appreciate His love for me. Because He does love me, I can't help but to have love for Mama. I can do everything in my power to love the way that God loves.

Overcoming: Discovering Rhonda

Ecclesiastes 7:8a says in the New Living Translation, *"Finishing is better than starting."* I bear witness to this fact. I know beyond any doubt that the things that are stored up for me are worth all of the heartache that I have endured during my early years. Discovering all of who Rhonda is has not been a simple task. Layers and layers of life's situations have not only been peeled back, but there is still yet more peeling to do, more to experience, more to overcome, more to encounter, more of God to experience and more to give. In fact, there is more ahead of me than what is behind me. All of my previous years and experience have been leading me to this dimension in my life. I chose not to be bitter about what I've been through, I choose to continually get better. Everyone has storms and difficulties, the question is, how do you navigate them?

I have the understanding now that every intricate detail of my life has been divinely orchestrated by the Creator to shift me, mold me, and make me into the person that He alone designed for me to be. I have always been different from most people that I knew, and now I know why. It wasn't because I was so much better than anyone else, it was because of the plan that God has for me. There are times that the storm is so fierce and the warfare is so great that I have to remind myself of Romans 8:28 that says, "And we know that all things work together for the good of them that love God, to them who are called according to his purpose." And I have to remember that in the end, I win. Truthfully I am who I am because of what I have endured and because of this fact, although painful, I would do it again because I know that there was and is purpose for it all. I have been encouraged several different times that, "it will all make sense in the end."

I attended a conference in California and on October 10, 2019, I received a prophecy that again changed the trajectory of how I viewed myself. God made me on purpose and some of the characteristics that I don't care too much about are the very things that He placed in me intentionally. I am not boasting in myself, I am boasting in the LORD. There is something inside of me that won't allow me to accept things that are half done or done haphazardly. I also somehow end up with people looking to me as the person in charge, even when I'm not. God placed a level of authority within me that shows up just because it wants to! I honestly attributed my intolerance of certain situations as an inadequacy, but I now realize that it is a part of my makeup, my DNA. I carry a level of authority and I'm learning to navigate it. The things that I considered as failures were not failures, they were set ups and even opportunities to grow and mature spiritually. God sees the value in me in spite of my quirks and idiosyncrasies.

I am Abba's pearl discussed in Matthew 13:45-46. I am the one the kingdom of heaven sought and then sold their belongings to buy. Jesus paid the cost for this pearl's redemption, salvation, and deliverance. This pearl is priceless. It matters not what others may say or think about my value as a woman, as a mother, or even as a daughter. I know that God values me, the person He created and the person that He loves. I am still discovering all of who Rhonda is. She is evolving daily into the woman that God created her to be. She has already been through so much and that which was sent to destroy her only made her more determined than ever to succeed.

There are gifts, mantles, and anointings that God placed in me before I was born. While I was completely unaware of what God was doing, even before I was conceived, He chose me as a vessel to carry His glory and to carry His Word. That fact alone continues to blow my mind on a regular basis. In the King James Bible, Matthew 22:14 says, "For many are called, but few are chosen." It's not that He doesn't call, but very few answer and say yes. He chose us, but we have to choose Him! I choose Him. I said and continue to say, yes. God has placed gifts inside of me that my yes will, through the power of the Holy Spirit, help His people get healed, delivered, set free and made whole. I am excited for what is ahead!

As a child, my mother was not affectionate, I didn't get hugs or kisses like that but God has positioned me to give to others that which I did not receive as a child. Certainly as an adult more hugs and I love yous were spoken and initiated, so there is yet beauty for ashes. There is inside of me a genuine capacity to love those that I am assigned to. I cannot love them on my own but through Him all things are possible. There has been betrayal and abandonment but through it all, He won't allow me to let certain people go. We are to look at Jesus as our example, so I can't help but see how He came to give His life to people that rejected Him and hung Him on a cross. He went through so much for humanity; how can I disobey? His commandment to love as He loves. I don't always get it right and I'm thankful for His forgiveness and restoration.

Key Takeaways from Discovering Rhonda

What you have read so far is a lot to process and, honestly, it's been a lot to even go through. But there have also been discoveries and invaluable lessons learned. Prayerfully, these takeaways will benefit others who may be in the same or similar situations.

1. *There is nothing wrong with you.* One of the first things that I discovered on this journey of overcoming rejection is the actual fact that there is absolutely nothing wrong with me. I am fearfully and wonderfully made and there is Kingdom purpose for and in my very existence. I admonish you, the reader, to not let the swirl of doubt and fear surrounding you influence you otherwise. I did not understand the "whys" of some of the things that happened and truth be told, some of it I still do not understand. God did not tell me that I would understand. He told me to "lean not to my own understanding" per Proverbs 3:5b, so all I have to do is trust The One who has the plan and that is God. Your life has value. Your life has meaning. So please do not let the wind distract you from hearing His voice and from receiving what God has in store for you.

2. *Accept you.* Another nugget is to get free, and in order to be free, we have to accept the good, the bad, and the ugly of where we are and who we are. We also have to accept where the people in our lives are spiritually, emotionally, and mentally. We have to face the truth, and in some cases, confront the truth. Is it always easy to confront the truth? No, it is not. But it is absolutely necessary for your freedom and spiritual well-being. My hurtful truth is that my mother rejected me and yet still at times

rejects not only me but the fruit of my womb as well. I will only know the real reason why if the Holy Spirit reveals it to me. But her rejection does not define who I am. God does the defining and my job is to believe what He says about me and to come into agreement with it.

3. *Let go.* This may seem elementary, but let the past go! Let go of the hurt and fear; the anger, the rage. Let go of wanting an apology. Let go of the bondage of carrying the past around with you everywhere you go. If you don't let it go, it will contaminate your future. My future is so much brighter than my past. Yours is, as well! Don't believe the lies that are whispered into your ears. Holding onto unforgiveness, bitterness, pain and the like only hinders your growth. Forgiveness is not just a biblical principle, there is so much freedom in forgiving, letting go of the hurt, and moving on to the better that is before you. I promise you that there is light at the end of the tunnel but there is a constant moving forward required of you in order to reach that light. There's a constant going forward in the tunnel even when hell seems to be breaking loose all around you. Forgiveness includes forgiving yourself for anything that is holding you hostage. A decision, a conversation that didn't go well, whatever it may be; forgive yourself as well as those that hurt you.

Overcoming: Healing from the Top Down

Healing can happen instantaneously but for the most part,

it is a slow process. It is also somewhat of a painful process that involves confronting the trauma that tried so hard to destroy you. Feelings thought to be long forgotten resurface with a vengeance and demand an audience. Reliving the past hurts as though the slights and jabs happened yesterday because we are not healed from the trauma of the situation. Forgiveness comes but we must also get inner healing and sometimes deliverance from the trauma. Healing actually begins from the inside out. But that inner healing starts at the top. It starts with God above. He touches the heart and mind and the healing is made manifest by the fruit of the Spirit you exhibit. The healing then becomes evident in the rest of our lives through the works of our hands and by our walk with God.

One of the first steps in receiving my healing was to know and recognize God's love. His love is so pure that it transcends anything in this natural realm. God's love is supernatural and it takes a level of faith to not only believe that He loves me, but also to actually accept His free gift of love. His love looks like sending His Son Jesus to die on the cross for my sins. His love looks like Him forgiving me time and time again when I've missed the mark or made a mistake. His love accepts me because He created me. His love finds me and picks me up when I am down. To know the love of God is to know His Son Jesus the Christ. He even encourages me in His Word. Psalm 27:10 says, *"When my father and my mother forsake me, Then the LORD will take care of me."* So then I am assured that everything I need can be found in my Father's love and compassion.

Healing is then a mental exercise. Deliverance can take place fully once we acknowledge, confront, and work through the pain of our past and the pain of the present. It reminds me of the meetings for Alcoholics Anonymous or a similar support group. The first step is to acknowledge and voice that there is a problem. Where denial is present, healing can never take place. Confronting past hurts stirs up the feelings all over again because complete healing never took place. We just covered things up with a bandaid. These bandaids take on the form of so many things, a smile, alcohol, anger, sarcasm, overworking, looking for love in all the wrong places. The list is endless but healing can begin by taking that first one step. The past will still be painful but we have to press past the pain.

Years ago my daughter had to have a tonsillectomy. The main instruction was to have her drink something several times an hour. If she didn't, the area where the tonsils were removed would not heal properly. Now mind you swallowing was very painful.

"Mama, it hurts!" she cried as I encouraged her to drink.

"I know it does but there is healing in the pain. If you don't drink the liquids, then you won't heal properly."

So while confronting the past and even the present brings back old emotions and reopens wounds, healing will not take place if we don't become intentional about confronting it. And once we take that big step, then we have to work through it. There are trauma counselors, pastors who operate in deliverance, therapists, psychologists and the like who are experts in helping us work through the trauma that causes so much pain. Sometimes all it takes is a really good friend who you can trust to listen, be non-judgemental, and give wise counsel. I am thankful for the Holy Spirit who gives us wisdom and assists us in every stage of life that we go through. Working through the pain is a slow process and it cannot be rushed. It takes time to dig and uncover all of the layers that we build up to hide our pain and the dysfunction related to the pain.

Pride sometimes rears its ugly head to try and deceive us into thinking that we are okay, when the reality is we are far from being okay. I know we all may have heard the saying, "It's okay not to be okay, but just don't stay there." But it's true. Therapy, counseling, deliverance, prayer and the like are all tools that are available to help us heal and not stay there. Again, we must admit there is a problem and seek help and guidance from trusted pastors, leaders, and healthcare professionals. We also have to be in the right mental space to receive the healing that God has for us. Whether you confess to being a believer or not, God loves us enough to not leave us in the condition that we are in.

Speak Life

"Death and life are in the power of the tongue, and those who love it will eat its fruit," says Proverbs 18:21. I truly don't think that some people realize that speaking negativity is speaking death. Speaking life into our situations means that I may not see the outcome yet, but I believe that everything is going to be alright. Things will get better. I will be healed of trauma and rejection. It is so important to have the right people around you. We don't need people around us that enable our dysfunction. Rather, we need those that will tell us the truth about ourselves in love, even when it doesn't feel good. Speaking positively looks like I'm going to speak it until I see it. I can say with assurance, *I know that God wants me healed and He has made provision for me to be healed. I will walk in my healing.* These are examples of speaking life over yourself and your situation.

It started at the top with God's love, a change in my mind and my mouth. Then my heart healed as I released the hurt and pain. I allowed the void to be filled with God's love for me. Forgiveness is not always an easy task for minor things, let alone those deep heart wounds. It begins with small steps that gradually increase to bigger steps. When we forgive, we have to be prepared to forgive again. This means when that hurt, pain, anger or frustration rears up, we make the conscious decision to open our hearts and our mouths and say, "I forgive you for hurting me, betraying me, manipulating me" or whatever the case may be. There is no pre-determined number, we have to forgive as many times as it takes until we are free. I don't have to make a grand announcement. I have to just do what I need to do to receive my healing and that is to forgive.

Deliverance

Deliverance is last because it's not a ministry that every church participates in. However, it is crucial to overcoming and healing from spiritual battles and warfare. I'll come back to this shortly.

The spirit of rejection is an unclean spirit sent to distract us from our purpose, assignment, ministry, joy, peace and everything that God desires for us to have during our lifetime. Unclean spirits have to be cast out. This process is called deliverance and it is nothing to be fearful of. Deliverance can happen through praying, and deliverance can even happen through our tears as we release these things. Counseling and therapy aid in deliverance as well.

However, we need faith to believe that God wants us to be free and that He has set us free. We need tools, like coping skills provided by pastors, counselors and therapists to be able to manage our emotions. We also need the Word to govern our behavior and bolster our faith.If I don't believe that I'm free, I will act and behave as if I'm not free. This goes back to what we said about healing being a mental exercise. My mind has to be renewed and my brain has to be retrained to not react the same way that it used to.

Now, let's talk further about deliverance. Please take the next thing that I am going to say very seriously. Deliverance must only be done by someone who operates in a strong deliverance ministry. This ministry is powerful and effective for someone who truly wants to be set free from rejection or any other unclean spirit that wants to destroy us. Every believer according to the Word of God has been commissioned by Jesus to cast out demons. In Matthew 10:8 Jesus commands the disciples to, "heal the sick, cleanse the lepers, raise the dead, and cast out devils." The anointing is needed to be an effective deliverance minister. Deliverance is life changing but it must be maintained. It can be a "one and done" but after being delivered, the person must continue to renew their mind in the Word of God. They must stay connected to individuals who will love them through it all, but at the same time hold them accountable. To skip out on continually being filled and refreshed in the Word of God is to your detriment because scripture says,

"When an unclean spirit goes out of a man, he goes through dry places, seeking rest; and finding none, he says, 'I will return to my house from which I came.' And when he comes, he finds it swept and put in order. Then he goes and takes with him seven other spirits more wicked than himself, and they enter and dwell there; and the last state of that man is worse than the first." (Luke 11:24-26, NKJV)

To not fill up on the Living Water of God's Word is to leave room for the enemy to take up residency with his ugly friends.

A Final Word

THERE MUST BE AN EARNEST DESIRE to be free. I didn't want to live my life controlled by the whims of someone else. I couldn't allow what my mother or anyone else felt about me to determine my worth and value. Rejection could no longer be the tool used to subdue me and subvert God's plan for me. I am who I am and all that I am only by the grace of God. I choose to believe one of my go-to scriptures that help me manage difficult situations when I don't necessarily understand. That would, again, be Romans 8:28. "And we know that all things work together for good to those who love God, to those who are called according to His purpose." I believe this verse, first, because God said it, and secondly because my very life depends on me believing what God says in His Word.

I now know with certainty, despite my experiences, who I am. I am an overcomer. I am victorious. I am His chosen. And He loves me regardless of what anyone else has to say about me. I may have been Mama's Girl, but I am most certainly Abba's Pearl. Though once hidden, I've been found to be of great value. He loves me unconditionally. It is in this unconditional love of God that I found the strength to act, the boldness to say no, the peace that only He can give, the confidence to trust in my abilities, and so much more. He gave me wholeness, He restored and continues to restore me daily. It is a continual thing, not just one time. As the Psalmist David wrote in Psalm 23, "Yea, though I walk through the valley of the shadow of death, I will fear no evil; For You are with me; Your rod and Your staff, they comfort me." The things that I have gone through in that valley of the shadow of death did not look or feel good, but they worked out for my good.

I mentioned earlier that healing starts at the top with God and infiltrates the mind and heart, becoming evident in the works of our hands and our walk with God. I am now walking in the purpose for which God created me. I am still learning and growing and maturing at an accelerated pace. I have not reached the full level of where I am going, but I am on my way.

There is so much freedom in trusting God's will for your life, even when you can't see the way and it doesn't make natural sense.

I encourage everyone who reads this book to allow God to break everything off of you that hinders you and slows down your progress in completing your assignments. I daresay, it's in the midst of allowing God to break the chains of bondage that your purpose and thus, your assignments, will become even more clear. Seek and find the healing that He promises and be assured that you are of great value to Him despite the actions of others. You are His, and He wants you to have everything that He has for you. This includes peace, joy, a sound mind, and abundant life.

~ Meet the Author ~

Rhonda Joyce is a servant of the Most High God. She desires for everyone to come into the knowledge of Jesus Christ as their own personal Lord and Savior. She resides in Spring Hill, TN with her family.

www.ingramcontent.com/pod-product-compliance
Lightning Source LLC
Chambersburg PA
CBHW020326130626
46549CB00003B/1044